PUPPY LOVE

Written by
Christine Simpson

Illustrated by
Judith Orner Bruce

*To Stephanie –
Lots of puppy love
to you! Fondly,
Chris & Duke*

Paulist Press
New York   Mahwah, N.J.

To Bryan, who forgot to buy me a baseball ticket
— C.S.

Text copyright © 1998 by Christine Simpson

Illustrations copyright © 1998 by Judith Orner Bruce

Book design by Cheryl Nathan

Illustrations by Judith Orner Bruce

Library of Congress Cataloging-in-Publication Data

Simpson, Christine.
    Puppy love / written by Christine Simpson; illustrated by Judith Orner Bruce.
       p. cm.
    Summary: All kinds of children learn how to treat others by watching puppies express their unconditional love.
    ISBN 0-8091-6652-6 (alk. paper)
    [1. Dogs--Fiction. 2. Conduct of life--Fiction. 3. Stories in rhyme.] I. Bruce, Judith Orner, ill. II. Title.
    PZ8.3.S6125Pu 1998   98–13306
    [E]--dc21   CIP
                                           AC

Published by Paulist Press
997 Macarthur Boulevard
Mahwah, New Jersey 07430

Printed and bound in Hong Kong

Puppies love boys and girls of color
And twins identical to each other.

Pups romp with kids with hearing aids
And Asian girls with long, thick braids.

Freckled boys with hair of red
Are great to snuggle with in bed.

Challenged kids, both big and small—
Pups don't care—they love them all!

Pups like rides in chairs with wheels,
And roller skates get similar squeals.

A Native American boy or girl
Is welcome in a puppy's world.

Kids with glasses,
crutches, braces
Bring happiness to
puppies' faces.

Children with unusual names
Are included in all the games.

Straight hair, curly hair, eyes of blue—
Red birthmarks are lovable too.

And kids with hats or violins
Win puppies' feelings deep within.

Heavy, skinny, short, or tall—
Pups don't care—just bring
a ball!

A stick is great when used for fun,
But raised in anger, scares each one.

An unkind word, a scowl, a hit,
A tug on the tail matter quite a bit.

Or being told to go away—
They cannot join; they cannot stay.

But a gentle smile or pat on the head
Steals a puppy's heart instead.

To be included as a friend
Wins a dog's love in the end.

Just watch puppies when they roam
With other dogs around your home.

Long hair, short legs, polka dots,
Mixtures, plume tails matter not.

Even a pup that's lost a leg
Joins in the fun without a beg.

All types of dogs play with the
crowd. It's OK to be different—
it's allowed.

Pups are smart.
They know what counts.
The way you treat them
makes them bounce.

It isn't the size or the shape of your nose
Or the language you speak or your style
of clothes.

Your religion, race or particular cause
Matters not to those with paws.

It's the warmth and the glow and the
gold in your heart
That puppies respond to from the start.

What do puppies know that we do not?